STONES

(a deconstruction of Zion)

David Schein

Fomite
Burlington, VT

ISBN-13: 978-1-959984-85-6

Fomite
58 Peru Street
Burlington, VT 05401

09/14/2024

STONES was originally performed in a workshop production at The Home for Contemporary Theater and Art in NYC. Running for four performances, January 29 - 30 and February 5 - 6, 1990 on a double bill with Schein's short play, PAGANS. STONES was directed by Michael Keens and performed by the author.

Yiskadol va yiskadosh shemeh rabbaw...Amen.
Vah amrah...ummm... amrah devaraw keerosay
vvvvvvvah...uhhh.... yamleek keerosay...ahhh...
shit...uh, vah chay yay chone ooh vah what? What?
I can't do this. I shouldn't do this. Strike me dead.
I've never ever been there. My folks go there all
the time, they're there now, but I'm not going to
visit them. I'm going to Germany instead. There's a
vacuum there that needs me, it calls to me, "Come
back, come back, we're sorry." I guess I don't want
to displace anybody. From where? From the back of
my mind where it's been going on for years. I've been
pre-*occupied*.

Israel – Is-it-real?

Israel – Is-it-real?

I know what would happen: I get on a plane, the
security is unbelievable, they look up my ass, take
apart my shaver to look for plastiques in the tines,
and I'm thankful, I don't want to be a body part left
over from some political pyro's PR stunt. Of course
they put me right next to this young Hassid, you
know the kind that look like they grew up yesterday
and immediately became your barely adolescent
great-grandfather, the one in the top hat in the
photograph, the Holy One from Dnipropetrovsk,
who was too religious to work, they said, and who
eventually opened a bar in Brooklyn. There's a whole
squad of these baby-faced beardos on the plane, and
it's strange, none of them are sitting together.

Now we take off, CHOOOOOOOOOOOM,
Rabbi Elvis next door, he doesn't want to make
conversation, he won't laugh at my bomb joke, he
shakes his head and mumbles to himself, sound like

he's praying in Hebrew, "Shoh Ney Vochker Vaster,"
which is all I remember from Hebrew School,
"Johnny Fuckerfaster," Hershy Cohen hissing
dirty jokes over my shoulder and firing spitballs at
Steinlauf's fat ass whenever he turned to work on the
board.

Steinlauf, Steinlauf, Steinlauf. I hadn't thought about
him in years.

"Take it easy on him," my folks said, "he had it
really tough."

"But he's so fat and boring," I said, "he's like the
God of Boredom."

"He didn't get enough to eat in Auschwitz. Now he's
making up for it."

I didn't care, he still bored the shit out of me. Six
hours of Hebrew School for four years, while the
Catholic kids only had Catechism once a week.
Archaic bible Hebrew, taught by rote which I didn't
understand and had only learned to pronounce.

But it wasn't the language that I could only parrot, it wasn't the God that I didn't believe in, or the fact that I wasn't going to get as much cash as the rest of the kids if I stuck it out until my Bar Mitzvah and the big day came, it was my first and last Bar Mitzvah instruction at Steinlauf's apartment that ended my career as a Bad Jewish Boy, it was his apartment, the dingy two rooms on Archibald Street, it was his poverty, it was his pathetic marginality that made my skin crawl. Here was this huge Yeshiva bucher ripped out of burning Europe to pass the eternal flame onto me, a Child of Disney, Son of Walt and the Holy Mouse, who could see nothing by the light of his sputtering ghetto candle but the outline of a futile existence. I gave up on Judaism that week and took up Nordic religion instead. Skiing.

I fall asleep over the ocean and SPRANNNNNG, SPRANNNNNG, jew-jew-jew- jew-jew-jew-jew-jew-jew- jew, I wake up fast. GUNSHOTS. People are yelling. The Hassids are out of their chairs firing machine guns, their coats are open, their belts are festooned with grenades. Off with their phony sidelocks, they throw their hombreros into the aisle, and underneath are checkered handkerchiefs. My neighbor is a SHE. Yikes. She tears off her beard and jams a gun barrel into my cheek, screaming, "We are the Holy Daggers of Mohar, who are the Jews here?"

Now that's kind of an anti-Semitic remark, I'm thinking, "Who are the Jewish people here?" would be less offensive, or, "Who here is Jewish?" When goys call a Jew "a Jew" you know there is no love.

And, what's the prize if you check the box? A check? A stone? Fifteen minutes of fame? The Bar Mitzvah money I never got? Hey, I'm an athi-ana-theasiest, you know, Church of No Pain? Eclectic, like most of you, a bit of Hindu, a pinch of Voodoo, Buddha-Butoh, OK, yeah, you got me, I yam a SEMI. TIGHT. ASS.

Oh, Lord, there's gonna be a lot of skin hanging from the luggage rack, half the plane looks lke Haddasah bingo night on a binge. Me, I can pass, no problem Scheiny German name, blue eyes, button nose, sandy hair, they won't pick me, the racists. But then I'll have to watch as they torture the Steinlaufs, tattooed as they are by their Mediterranial darkness and their old-country Westchester accents. I don't know if I can take it. Jesus wouldn't have watched. He would have stood up and turned the other cheek right in their face. But I'm not like him, I'm a chickenshit. And there's a place for chickenshits. We can observe. Bear witness. Sell the story.

Of course, her X-ray eyes detect a significant lack of foreskin beneath my seatbelt buckle and she immediately nails ME. The rest of the passengers, somehow not one of them is Jewish. No, the Hadassah ladies are really a bevy of Palestinian grandmothers returning from a fundraising tour of the Holy Land sponsored by the Pistachio Nut Growers of America and the rest of them are *Mexican*, bible scholars from a seminary in Guanajuato on a pilgrimage to the shrine of the Holy Ghost. Soon to be me.

Well, somebody's got to be the Jew. OK, I accept, I'm honored, Thank you.

Your turn next life and that means never-ending Hebrew School, six hours a week for at least four years & Junior Congregation and Johnny Fuckerfaster too. You can be the next kibble bite for the purebred ethnic God Dog. Get him, Abu, infidel Shite.

They make everyone else get to the back of the plane and push me towards the door. Oh Lord, she's opening it, Jesus, doesn't she realize she'll be sucked out with me? She heaves at the steel bar that seals us from the sky and it begins to move, alarms go off, red bulb eyes blink, the door flies open and... thwooooop; a cloud pulls my face off and I follow, falling, too heavy for Heaven I guess, but I'm not alone, there's an angel with an automatic far above, floating like a spider in the blue. "Some, sunny day, some sunny day, we'll meet again, some sunny day."

Below me the Land of Milk and Honey is rising. I'm

gasping, the original Calestine of yore, orchards, vineyards, the beautiful postcard from Auntie Eve, the way the dry forest comes down to the sea, the beautiful forest reaching for me and I wonder, will I be impaled up the ass by the same tree my parents bought me years ago for Israel? Ayyyyleeeeeeahhhh! I fall free, spread my eagle and glide past dun-colored hills into a valley that gets bigger and closer every second, fields, orchards, a silo, the sun's reflection gleaming in an open holding tank, my shadow growing larger in its scarlet pool. I ball up for impact to meet it; the final me.

Sheh-mah

Sha-dow

SUH-PLASH.

Shadow is wet, Shadow is red. I am preserved. Boreh pree hagofen. Blessed is the wine.

It IS the land of miracles. 30,000 feet later, I fall the final foot, smashing through grapes that suck my

shockwaves into a bruised crimson jelly. I, the fallen
Jew, can't find, can't find, the bottom, am floating
in the mash, wriggling every digit to see what still
works, my eyes sealed with grapeskin, lips caked
with sweet dregs. I flounder for any hard edge, find
one, haul myself up on shaking arms to the rim of
the vat. And there she is. The Promised. Cuious.
Land.

And there *she* is, picking through the rubble of
a recently ruined house. She fell faster, landed
thousands of years before me, with her goats, her
moustache and her slingshot.

Shalom. Peace. God is great. Allah is great. Jesus is
the bomb. We'se all great.

I have survived. So fuck me gently.

Oh oh. Three mad nomads appear, then a crowd,
all in identical "No Problem" t-shirts, all bearing
fistfuls of stones. I make tracks from the vat;
the dust puffs up around me as they chase me

through a hole in a fence into a lemon grove. I zag left, swing up into a tree and hide in the thorny green. They run right under me, their voices fade in the distance. Whew. I wait to make my move. "Jewjewjewjewjewjewjewjew," semi-automatic screams. They all come running back pursued by soldiers in riot gear and newsmen who shoot them with video cameras. I wait some more, then, out of the tree, broken-field run, kangaroo hopping from tree to tree through fences and orchards, vineyard and plantations all grown out of the barren desert with heart-breakingly, breath-taking advanced technology, until I come to an irrigation ditch by a deserted highway.

Mmmmmmmmmmmmmmmmmm. Diesels gowl in the distance. I fling myself into the ditch and land on A MAN WITH SUCKING CHEST WOUND. He moans. I touch his forehead. With his last breath he spits in my face. Trucks speed by, full of singing prisoners and their guards. Night falls. The body grows cold beneath me.

Camouflaged by the long shadows I scramble up
dry terraces of olive groves to the top of a ridge.
Searchlights slice the sky, their arcs spoking out from
the barbed wire hub of a settlement on a mountain
to the east, while to the west – turrets and spires
silhouetted by the dusk. Ah yes, the Holy City;
Benarestan Meccaville, Romeyoto, Vegas, Nashville,
Yerushaliyum. One day in…..

Not tonight. I'm too beat. It's been a big day…and
I need light for the rest of this, so I make a bed out
of the only available material, stones, curl myself
against the hot desert wind and fall into…

"That's a load of crap."

"You should be ashamed for talking that way…"

Yes, a dream of…ah…it's a family argument which,
in my family, we call "dinner." Aunt S. and Uncle B.
have cooked up their favorite supper of slurs. The
hors d'oeuvre is Roast Kid of Schwartzer ("They
don't look after their own children") and the first

11

course is an all-too recognizable Palestinian dish ("You don't negotiate with animals"). It looks like the entrée is going to be ME and I'm not having any.

"You think that? So how do you call yourself a Jew?"

I want to throw up. "Look, I don't call myself a Jew, you call me a Jew, they call me a Jew, I call myself "*myself*" and everyone answers. And it's useless fighting, we're never going to agree...so could you please pass the salt? This wound's a little too healed."

Ding dong. It's the doorbell. Saved by the bell. "I'll get it."

Hey, it's a Mormon in a tie, boy, does that get my alignment straight in a flash.

"Thanks, but I'm a Jew. We killed Christ and we'd do it again. Have a blessed day. Goodbye."

SLAM! And don't you laugh Uncle B. I eat Dog. I

burn the Flag, and I'd step on the Torah too, Zayde, just a little, softly, I'll wear slippers, not to hurt, with great respect, but just to make sure that it's dead, that it's just words, that the "law" won't rise up and kill anyone in my name. So I'm not going to fight your battles. My battle's with you. With anybody who takes it literally. I'M NOT SIGNING UP.

Yeah, I can just see it. Off to Israel go I, ostensibly to visit M & P and the last you hear I've fallen in with an ancient landgrab hustle operating under the name of Adonoi Inc. You get a picture postcard from some West Bank Belson, me in a barbed wire tallas handing out gift-wrapped bricks to smiling tearful Palestinans who can't wait to launch them in my direction. And we feel the same way and we've got bigger bricks so let the air-games begin. Swallowed by Israel...that's all she wrote. Thank you Adolph, thank you Aaron.

Have I lost you? Obviously I've lost myself, I'm trapped in a disa-gression, crying in my sleep on a

13

ridgetop and a pillow of stones. Above me loom the spires and turrets of…better wake up and move this epic before it runs aground in the eternal sands.

Nininininininininininininininining. It's dawn. There's a VW Bug with its motor running by the foot of my bed. A road winds from the ridge to an armed checkpoint at the Gate of the City and…there she is! Looking down at me, friendly now, like a Palestinian Unitarian, dressed in her business suit for her job across the Zion Line, and she's beckoning me, she wants me to come along, to carpool with her into a non-polarized future, to give a firm but gentle finger to the penalties for collaboration from both sides. I must. I do…enter her Bug and ride with her to cross the Great Divide.

I can't help but falling, she's so beautiful with her Liz Taylor moustache and maple-mocha eyes, yes and we can do it, for we are young and our love is our duty; we will spawn a new race of Jewrabs, and all the hatred and fear and the angel/devils of our otherness will twine together in the DNA strands of our multi- denominational offspring and they will be stronger for the traumas embedded in their genes. I smile at her, I place my hand over hers on the knob of the stick-shift, but she flings it off, glares at me and guns the car on two wheels around a hairpin. Ah yes, I see, she will not be a slave to potential empathy, it's nothing personal, it's because they took her brother away and broke his arm, because they tear-gassed her family and blew up their house, but if it's not personal, it's patronizing, so yes, I will cross the border to honor her boundary, and in my mind, make "hers" mine, my brother, my parents, our house.

She pulls up a hundred yards before the checkpoint.

"Get out of the car," she says. I didn't know she spoke English.

"But we were just getting to know each other." She pulls a revolver out of her blouse and sticks in my third eye. I do what she says.

"Will I see you again?"

"FOREVER," she screams and gungungunguns
the motor. I'm left in a cloud of exhaust as she barrels
that bug of a carbomb right into the checkpoint
guardhouse, BARRRROOOOM, blowing herself
and 20 or 30 soldiers , a hundred odd tourists and
the dreams of a couple of millions of my old Hebrew
School buddies right out of the Promised Land.

For nothing personal, I'm thinking as I float over the
ruined checkpoint, ambulances wailing far below,
propelled by the force of the explosion into heart of
the City that bears my name.

The City of David.

Landing lightly on my feet, my Reeeboks pound the
ancient flagstones as I make my way to the Sacred
Plaza, through another armed checkpoint into the
Holy Yard. I'm following a procession of women,
these are the Torelles, the Women of the Torah;
they wear long skirts and prayer shawls, and carry

the Holy Scroll, the Word of Words, the Law of Laws, the Book of Books. Between them and the Wall of Wails waits a taunting mass of black-hatted payessed/bearded men, arms linked to form a human chain to block the women's way. I recognize their leader from the magazine covers, it's Rabbi Khomeni, self-styled Enforcer of the Jealous Gawd Squad and he yells at the women, "Go to the churches and pray there where you belong," while the Ortho-Mobodoxy snort and flip their sidelocks like mad stallions in the spring.

But nothing deters the Women of the Torah. In a soft phalanx, spearheaded by soldiers who force the Ultras to either side, the women, singing in their prayer shawls, proceed past a barricade, through the section cordoned off and posted, "For Female Worship Only" and into the forbidden patio of Gawd's Men's Room.

The Hasids are incensed. They want the women away from the Wall, the stain of their sacrilege expunged. Stones are thrown, Clubs rise, come down and all hell breaks loose at the Holy of Holies. Welcome to the Wall War, it's a blockbuster bone-breaker that's only been running for thousands of years, ever since the Chosen people left the Land of Bondage and kicked the Can-aanites outa the Land of Milk and Honey in the name of the Lord and Lebensraum, an epic starring Rabbi Khomeini as "Joshua Fitdeebattle," except instead of a Prophet with Trumpet he's a Fanatic with a Folding Chair which he flings over the barricade onto the heads of the women, sending them sprawling. His followers storm the barricade to wrest the Sacred Word from the Unclean Hands of the Torah Gals, but undaunted, the women sing louder, dig their fingernails deeper into the Law until it bleeds, until the Israeli Police bring down their batons on the Hasid's hard headed Hombergs. Finally Gawd appears as Himself and lets forth a punishing rain of tear gas upon the multitudes, and I, caught up in the spirit, am moved to tears and join the cast, appearing as Shepherd Dave, a simple lad with his flock and his sheep, drawn, from his flute-playing, into the horror of battle.

Action: I grab a burly Philistine by the beard and swing him around. He seizes my arm and his overcoat slides up. I see the numbers on his wrist. I look into familiar eyes. It's STEINLAUF.

"You never paid attention in class. You grew up to be a Nazi. MURDERER," he screams. I grab another handful of hair and whirl him into a fog of tears. Everybody's crying at the Wailing Wall. I'm blinded, gasping for salvation. My fingertips find a face in prayer. It bites my hand.

Shemah Shamir Sharon Shalom Auschwitz Belson Amen.

Shemah Shamir Sharon Shalom Begin's bygones begin again.

Shemah Shamir Sharon Shalom Auschwitz Belson Amen.

Shemah Shamir....

It's HER. Again. Reconstituted as tomorrow's post atomic Princess of the Way to Come. Esther Von Einstein. She's got a Mohawk haircut and a black leather tallas, she's got the Torah in a stroller and my hand in her teeth as she wheels it and pulls me away from the Brawling Faithful.

"Quick," she says, "Put this on." She gives me a blindfold.

The minute the black cloth kisses my face I see it clearly; I've been waiting for her, a woman like me. She has memory and no history, reverence but no allegiance, and together, yes, out of our loins we will beget a tribe that has no identifying characteristics, a tribe that can stay lost. And we will beat our car bombs into blenders and mix our stones with sand and lime to build gorgeous third-world beach-front apartments where we will sit on our patios over a turquoise sea, drinking local wine out of long-stemmed glasses, and after having violent political disagreements we will go to bed and make love as if it didn't matter, nothing mattered.

"Why this?" I ask straining to see through the black cloth in a momentary lapse of belief.

"It is a Yamika for the eyes," she says.

"And this?" As she ties my hands behind my back.

"Philacteries, they're your Tefillen."

"Am I a hostage?"

"It's for your own protection. This way, no one will notice you. You'll fit in here."

Wheeling the Torah before us, we leave the square. Now we're on a busy street. A car pulls up. "Get in," she says, guiding me into the trunk. A needle slides into my thigh. She lays the Torah on top of me.

"Will I see you again?"

"Shhhhh," she says. "First you have to wonder in the desert."

The trunk slams shut. I wrap my legs around the Torah and go under.

Another dawn falls rises purple on the Sinai. It's been three weeks since they dumped me here and every day's been a scorcher. The sun has burnt my blindfold into my face. I've eaten the rope that bound my hands and I've eaten the Torah too, chapter by chapter; The Song of Solomon went down easy but Leviticus stuck in my throat. I washed it down with water from a stone. Though now unbound and free to wander, still, I'm chained to an immovable history I'm not responsible for, and whenever I follow the chain of events back to its source it leads to myself. I'm self-interrogating constantly, doing the nice-cop, bad-cop switch but it seems that the interrogators keep changing their requirements so radically that my conciliations of one day are seen as defiance on the next, and though I've suspected all along that I'm bound to punished for whatever I say, for whoever I am trying to be, what I want to know is…is this it? Is waiting for the punishment the punishment?

Firewood is a real problem, those cold desert nights, brrrrrr. I've been slowly dismantling a dilapidated portapotty abandoned by an archaeological expedition and I'm down to its last splinters when... WHAM...three burly sabras appear from behind a sand dune, grab me, wrap me and my pitiful sticks in a Tallas, sling me over their shoulders as if I was a rug and bounce me over the desert chanting "Shabbas Shabbas no no no, on Shabbas Shabbas no no no..." A rescue? They're hungry? They're horny? Is this an initiation?

They round a sandstone escarpment and low and behold, before me is a magnificent tented city , a refugee camp struck like a miracle out of the desert. There's a big blue tent in the center of the encampment bedecked with CP (Chosen People) pennants. They throw me through the flaps, my sticks break against THE TABLETS at the feet of, it has to be, unmistakable with his white beard and his curley white locks, his eagle eye, his hawk nose, yes, it's the I — UH — TOLD — YUH — MOSE — ASS.

"Und vile duh children of Israel vere vondring in duh vilderness dey found a meyn gaddering sticks upon the Shabbas Day." He casts an accusing eye at my broken twigs. "And dey dat found heem gaddering sticks broung heem unto Moses and Aaron and unto all duh congregation. Und dey put heem in a room vich vas like a chail because it had not been declared vat should be done to him and den Gawd...SCHEIN YOU SHOOT VON MORE OF DOSE AND YOU VILL HEF TO TALK TO MR FROST...said unto Moses. Duh meyn shell surely be put to deatt; and all duh congregaytion shall stone heem with stones vittout duh kemp."

I ask the Mosatollah to make sure that my family gets my body immediately after the stoning ceremony so they can sit shiva and bury me but he says that regulations require that the priests perform an examination to make sure that I've been killed in the proscribed manner before my body can be released. I tell Mo if this happens I'm sure that Gawd will be very very very very very angry. The Ayamosha tells

Aaron to make a note of it.

They place me with my back against the cliff facing the crowd. The kids filter down to the first row, so that the adults can throw over their heads. They start taking practice shots but Mo tells them to wait for the signal. He asks me if I have any last words and boy, I've got a whole megillah's worth.

"Yes I picked up sticks on Saturday, but I don't think I oughta die for it. I mean, it's not like I befouled a well or anything I mean, how about some community service? What's appropriate? And while I've got your attention I just want to say that I don't think it's such a great idea to teach parables of institutionalized homicide to impressionable kids, you might want to think about that, and furthermore I think things have gone really to hell since we left the land of Egypt. Back then we had the feelin', we had the spirit, until the miracles happened and the waters parted and, just like what happens to a lot of grass-roots movements, things got authoritarian,

25

patriarchal and totalitarian and just because MOSES and AARON say that Gawd tells them to do this or that it doesn't mean that he really does…" Mo's getting nervous with the length of my palaver, but I know what I'm doing, I'm playing for time because I hear the rumble of motors in the distance and just as the Mosatollah gives his signal and a halo of stones assails my face, a phalanx of tanks crests the sand dunes and enter the compound. scattering the congregation.

BRRRRRRRRRRR. Big tank roars, up crack goes the hatch, a huge burly fatso squeezes out, sweat beads his brow, his glasses are fogged. It's COMMANDER STEINLAUF!

"I hope you've learned your lesson," he says. "There's only one way to deal with these animals."

Bong! A brick whistles by his face and bounces off the tank. Jewjewjewjewjewjew…he fires off a couple of rounds without aiming. The Mosatollah's tent bursts into flames

"Here." He throws me a club. "And here." He tosses a uniform.

"And here." He flips me a pistol that I throw back.

"I don't want your army," I say.

"So form your own." He squashes himself back into the tank and roars into a a flaming barricade. The kids behind it scatter, running in all directions. One heads for me, trips and falls. She gets up to one knee but before she can launch her cocktail I grab her wrist. It's HER, younger now, her beauty nascent, my twelve year-old bratty big sister, Saint Joan of Palestine, called by voices. She'll never apologize. She's always right. She looks up at me and her eyes sing "victory."

"Shoot me, your bullet bites back. Blow up my house, you'll make more stones. Beat me. My bones will break you."

She hands me a stone. It's every snowball, every hardball, every beer bottle I ever threw at a wall, fitting my hand. And it's perfect; the soldiers are silhouetted against the flame of the burning tires. Steinlauf's unmistakable, with his huge belly as he directs the round-up of the prisoners. My arm cocks back, but my heart...breaks...my arm. I can't. He's MY ghetto bucher, MY Zayde, a self I cannot stone.

She has no such qualms, lobs a good one, but TSEW TSEW TSEW...the photographer's flashbulubs catch her in mid-transgression. I grab her hand and we run, laughing scared into the desert darkness, as far as our legs can carry us, then walk into the chill of the Negev night, talking, holding hands, whispering secrets. Until we come to a semi-settlement at the desert's edge. She picks her way through the barbed wire to a small concrete house. We enter. It is full of children sleeping on pillows of stones. We lie down next to them.

BAM BAM BAM! 4 AM: Soldiers break down the door. They've got 8 X 11 glossies, evidence of our collective guilt. We're herded out of the house and, under TV lights, are forced to watch the "retribution." A little man in uniform, a submachine gun slung over his shoulder, high-knees it out the door on booted pony toes, nodding his head to a private count and BANG! The dynamite splits the house with an orange flash rumble, the walls spit out in four directions and the rooftiles dive into the billowing smoke. Backlit by the glow of furniture on fire, a radio explodes and burns with a green stinking flame.

The kids watch. They seem to enjoy the fire, the big whoosh and flicker of destruction, as if they know the flames of their burning house will serve to temper their anger, make it sharp and hard. Humpty Dumpty all fall down. Soon they will graduate from the School of Rocks and grow up to blow things up.

She's crying as they put her on the bus. A newsman tries to catch the tears with his camera but she flings her head away.

"Look at the camera. Hold that bandage up. Invite the world to fly with your stone. The kids in Mexico, New Delhi, Kyoto, Naples...we'll get them behind you, but you...but hey, not so defeated for Christ's sake, show some nobility, show some hostility." She spits at him. CLICK.

"Perfect."

For me they've got other plans. MOSSAD guys in jeans and shades take me downtown. They want to know who I'm working for. MOSSAD, intelligent intelligence, makes the CIA look like the Three Stooges. Keep this generation out of the ovens, bomb Beirut to make home safe, these agents of the refugees who've made more refugees, the *them or us guys*, MOSSAD, mo' sad, SO BAD and why? Well, if they were too young for Dachau their parents weren't, if they weren't wounded in four invasions, their brothers were, if their little sisters weren't blown up on their way home from school, there's always tomorrow. Unless *first strike and you're out.*

In other words these guys are not unsure of their
state of danger. They've been invaded four times,
they got the hate – it comes with the territory, just
like the kids in the camps, but they got F-14s to
throw back REAL BIG STONES, they're Jew-smart
and they wonder: Am I stupid?

They take me upstairs to the Big Boys. It's a
different kind of Hebrew School. No spitballs.
Sharon throws me around the office. Shamir leaves
no marks, Begin pumps milk into my stomach,
Mieir forces honey down my throat, then they
tell me: "Hey Mishpoca Man, stay lost, go back
to Newark go back to the Bronx, to East Los, to
Woodlawn, to your own refugee camps, leave ours
alone, boychick, goyshe Jew. You're one of ours
and we don't want you to get hurt, so get out,
because you're gonna get killed, not because you're
a Jew, it's nothing personal; it's a holy land dispute,
and if you find yourself on the wrong side of the
shifting lines in the sand, you're toast, and both
sides will burn you."

They toss me out in the street. It's the heart of the Old City. A stone bounces off my back. I'm running, chest on fire, from a gang of kids each with their "No Problem" t-shirts, each with a fistful of stones. I put on the steam, they're gaining. It's hopeless, there's no way to outrun them. I turn, yes, she's there, at the head of the pack, beckoning to me even as she hurls a brick at me. I know what she wants, she's wanted it all along and I have to, to save all my lives, finally cross over, my body runs on but my heart stands still, the mob catches up, my heart joins their tail, and I'm the mob, I'm the bomb, running after the Jew inside me. I quicken the pace, dodging into side streets, feinting into narrow twisted alleys, and I've almost caught up with myself when POP, the brick I throw hits the back of my head and I'm down, my boot kicks my ribs, my stick hits my face again and again and again, I'm blinded by blood, my head is finally and definitively split and then darkness delivers me from my own dilemma.

They take me from the hospital straight to my Folk's

flat. It's got a gorgeous view of the whole city, they tell me, which I'll see when they take the bandages off. Mom's just got back from Egypt with Aunt Buster, not a good trip because all Buster liked to do was shop and Mom liked to walk and sight-see and the two weren't compatible.

"She tried to buy the whole country. If she could have put Cheops in a box, she'd have shipped it home to Rochester." We laugh. My father and I avoid the politics. We don't want to get nasty. We'll save that for our letters. But they do mention Hebron, they used to love it, but now it's dangereous to go there. If the Intifada doesn't stone your car there's always the risk of some crazy settler opening up with his automatic. They complain about the fanatics fucking up the "social experiment" and lead me to the balcony so I can feel the warm sun on my face while they go in to make lunch.

I grope around on the ledge. There's a flower pot. I uproot the flower, dig down and find the drainage rocks and from the balcony of Mother's house I shoot a stone.

Into the air.

At anyone.

At all of it.

About the Author

David Schein has been positioned on the "cutting edge" for over fifty years as a jack of all genres and a professional "big mouth." He was born in Burlington, VT and raised in Burlington's Jewish community. He attended the University of Iowa and has lived and worked in the SF Bay Area, rural Quebec, NYC, Chicago, Tijuana, Ethiopia, Germany, and in the Southern Tier of western New York. In 2012 he returned to Burlington where he lives with his partner, Dana Block and their two parakeets, Jet Blue and Banana. *Stones* is Schein's fourth book published by Fomite Press, the other three being *My Murder and Other Local News* (performance poems), *The Adoption* (a novel about Ethiopia and America), and *TOKENS: A Play on the Plague*, (dialogue and lyrics from the award-winning opera written by Schein and composed by Candace Natvig English and Schein). To find out amore about David Schein's work go to davidschein.net.

Fomite

Writing a review on social media sites for readers will help the progress of independent publishing. To submit a review, go to the book page on any of the sites and follow the links for reviews. Books from independent presses rely on reader-to-reader communications.

For more information or to order any of our books, visit:
http://www.fomitepress.com/our-books.html

More plays and theater pieces from Fomite...

William Damkoeler — *The Occupant and Self-Storage*
Stephen Goldberg — *Screwed and Other Plays*
Vincenzo Lamartora/Michael Palma — *The Dimension of Loss*
Michele Markarian — *Unborn Children of America*
Hanna Eady and Edward Mast — *The Mulberry Tree and The Return*
David Schein — *My Murder and Other Local News*
David Schein — *Tokens: A Play on the Plague*